BREAKING THE POWER OF OF

Elizabeth Iheanacho

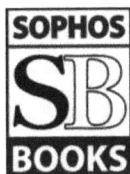

SOPHOS
SB
BOOKS

Breaking the Power of Fear
Copyright © 2024 by Elizabeth Iheanacho

Published by
Sophos Books
Croydon
CR0 0AZ
sophosandcredo.com

All scriptures, unless otherwise stated, are taken from The
Holy Bible, *New King James Version,* Copyright © 1982
Thomas Nelson. All rights reserved.
Scriptures marked:
KJV are from the *King James Version* of the Bible.
ESV are from The Holy Bible, *English Standard Version*,
Copyright © 2001 by Crossway.
NASB are from the *New American Standard Bible*, Copyright ©
1960, 1971, 1977, 1995, 2020 by The Lockman Foundation.
BSB are from the *Berean Standard Bible*, Copyright © 2020 by
Bible Hub.
LSB are from the *Legacy Standard Bible*, Copyright © 2021 by
the Lockman Foundation.
WEB are from the *World English Bible*.

ISBN 978-1-905669-25-7

Cover design by Tope Enoch
Printed in the United Kingdom

CONTENTS

Dedication		5
Appreciation		7
Preface		9
1.	What is Fear?	11
2.	Types of Fear	23
3.	How Does Fear Attach Itself To Us?	55
4.	God's Way	69
5.	Death Versus Life	75
6.	It's a Love Walk	81
7.	Divine Protection	85
8.	Don't Give Up the Fight	97

*To every person that has struggled
with the hold of fear and is looking for a way out;
to every person that desires the power to overcome the
grip that fear has over their lives, this book is for you!*

*To my daughters, Rebecca and Ann-Marie, who,
should the appearing of our Lord and Saviour Jesus
Christ tarry, will carry this message to
and beyond their generation.*

APPRECIATION

My deepest appreciation goes to the sweet Holy Spirit, who empowered, helped, and anointed me to write this book. I am nothing without His help and the love of my Saviour, Jesus Christ.

To my husband, Bishop Simon, for your support and your contribution, may God bless you.

To my two lovely daughters and son-in-law, who stood by me, encouraged me to keep going, and shared both wisdom and insight as I embarked on this journey, thank you.

To my parents, who are no longer with us, whose legacy lives on in the lives of my children and I, thank you. To my mother who, as a young widow, raised us after our dad passed. She was an example of strength, love, and hope, and she taught me to hold unto God and my faith. Thank you.

A special thanks to Rev Mrs Roma Williams, who dedicated her time and diligence, to proofread the initial text.

To all the members of *UK World Evangelism Church*, who have encouraged and stood by me in my ministerial calling. Thank you all!

PREFACE

This book draws inspiration from personal encounters and learned experiences from others. While it contains just a portion of the subject matter, there are many other writings bordering on fear that can help readers. If you are struggling with fear in any form, this book will serve as a stepping stone to freedom.

The subject matter is *fear*, and the force that makes it fully operational is *power*. Here, power refers to capacity, ability, strength, will, and authority that can influence a change in your way of thinking. It is a force, either negative or positive, that triggers compliance.

The title of this book, *"Breaking the Power of Fear,"* suggests that fear has inherent power, and this power can alter a man's life and destiny negatively. But the writer believes that the power of fear can be broken, such that we can gain access to walk in the God-centred life found in Christ Jesus. John 10:10 states: *"The thief comes only to steal and kill and destroy; I have come that they may have life, and have it to the full."*

I am convinced that your decision to pick up this book is not an accident; it is divinely orchestrated by the Holy Spirit. And as you flip through the pages, may you experience true freedom from fear.

CHAPTER 1

WHAT IS FEAR?

P eople commonly use the acronym, *fear*, to define and describe the nature of fear. This acronym stands for:

F: false

E: evidence

A: appearing

R: real

Taking this definition further, fear can be described as a false representation of a thought in the mind. As a diluted presentation, it distorts its true representation, and as a lie, it deceives the mind of the person captivated by it. Fear can also be a falsehood. When we believe a lie, we are deceived. It means our mind is darkened, and we cannot differentiate between a lie and the truth. It can also implies that we are illiterate on the subject matter.

The dictionary defines *fear* as an unpleasant, often strong emotion caused by the anticipation or awareness of danger. It suggests fear as a potent emotion that is so overwhelming that its power can incapacitate us. Scientists have researched the brain's response to danger and found that when we are afraid, our brain redirects energy to the part that triggers the fear, slowing down processes in other areas. This alteration can affect our ability to articulate how we feel or make rational decisions.

Whether you align with Christian beliefs or not, the more you succumb to fear, the more it becomes the decisive force that resonates in your conscious and subconscious mind. It hinders you from reaching your full potential and accessing your complete destiny in God. Consequently, fear becomes a distraction, causing anxiety, pain, failure, sickness, and an array of other limiting challenges.

It is crucial to recognise that fear does not emanate from God. If God is not the author of fear, then where does fear come from? The book of Genesis explains how God came down to the Garden of Eden to commune with creation, man. However, on this occasion, when He called out to Adam and Eve, their response was steeped in fear because they had disobeyed God. Their disobedience introduced fear into the world.

Fear is linked to the evil one. It is a product of the fallen nature of man. It is a remnant of our unregenerate selves before encountering Christ, our Lord and Saviour. To reiterate, fear is not of God and does not find its origins in Him. It can be likened to a gift. Just as one might handle a gift they dislike either by trashing it or rendering it useless, we can choose to approach fear the same way. I often tell my children that we tend to attract what we celebrate. And just as whatever we appreciate gains in value, what we devalue diminishes in worth.

Seeing fear as an undesirable gift will prompt us to discard the thoughts and imaginations associated with fear or frame them in a manner that empowers us to confront and overcome them.

God, in His benevolence, has granted each of us the willpower to either *reject* the spirit of fear or *embrace* its deadly influence. God has empowered us with the ability to thwart the attacks of the spirit of fear.

———◆———

Repeat this prayer, and confess it aloud:

I am a child of God and fear is not a gift from my father. I stand on the belief that living a life of fear is not the life intended for me. Today, I begin a new walk of love, life of faith, and a life free from fear, from now and moving forward in the name of Jesus. Amen.

———◆———

HOW HUMANS RESPOND TO FEAR

Our responses to fear often come in different forms, which include taking a flight, defending with a fight, freezing or fawning.

Response 1: Flight

When we perceive fear either through rejection or intimidation, it is natural to get angry. This anger is an emotional response that causes us to run away. The brain sometimes stirs up flight to ward off our position of fear. As previously stated, fear is a spirit, and spirits don't know distance, so we cannot run away from a spirit. Therefore, the best weapon to combat fear is not physical but spiritual. However, the unregenerate state of our mind can make us run from pillar to post. I have seen people change locations and jobs out of fear. Such moves only create temporary relief. After a while, the fear will find a way to enslave their minds again. The spiritual weapons needed to fight fear are the word of God and prayer.

> *"For the weapons of our warfare are not carnal, not a physical fight but they are mighty in God to the pulling down of every argument."*
>
> **2 Corinthians 10:4**

Whenever you sense fear, remember it is not physical, so attempting to combat it physically will only take you so far. You will be fighting the wrong person while the real person, Satan, stands at the corner watching in glee.

I remember as a child, when the civil war happened in my country, Nigeria, that my parents lost everything they had after the war. And with a family of nine children, things became hard. At mealtimes, my mother would set dishes of food for two groups. She would then sit to watch us eat while making sure that we all received an equal share of the food. I was a slow eater, and my younger sister, who could gulp down her food so quickly without chewing, handled me horribly. She would grab my food as I brought it to my mouth and eat it also.

This caused so much fear in me at every mealtime that, instead of putting up a fight, I would willingly hand over the food to her. I became afraid of eating anywhere in a group setting, afraid that everyone I ate with would demand my portion. I was afraid that my resistance would result in a fight that might choke me. This feeling of fear not only tormented me but also incapacitated my strength and ability.

This is an example of the flight nature, the fear of not being able to overcome, and acting incapacitated, when in truth, you may have the power to overcome. Instead of running off, stand your ground on the word of God and fight a good fight of faith. This suggests that there are good and bad fights. It is important to discern the best response for various situations.

Response 2: Fight

I used to listen to a song as a teenager in the 80s, whose lyrics state, "He who fights and runs away lives to fight another day." At that young age, it began to make more sense to me that life is a battle.

When the spirit of fear strikes a person, it can compel them to retaliate. Fear can thwart the divine vision for our lives, deceiving us into thinking we are incapable and dissuading us from fulfilling God's will. Engaging in a battle against fear is an endeavour that diminishes our physical well-being, posing challenges for maintaining good health.

We may engage in physical battles against fear because people we look up to sometimes label us as failures, so the fear of failure prompts us to fight. However, the Bible reassures us that we can do all things through Christ. Attempting to gain freedom by physically confronting a spiritual force – fear – will not grant us liberty. This is because our strength is limited but relying on the strength provided by God through the Holy Spirit allows us to fight and secure victory over fear. Romans 8:2 assures us that *"the law of spirit which is alive in Christ Jesus has set us free from the law of sin and death."*

As children, fear-oriented words are often spoken over our lives, and this can cause us to fight in the face of fear. We may unknowingly embrace fear, but to overcome it, consistently and intentionally affirm to ourselves countless times: "God has not given me the spirit of fear; I will not walk in fear." Teach your children to repeat this mantra from a young age, instilling in them the spirit of God, which signifies freedom from fear.

———◆———

Say this prayer:

Fear is not from God. I will fight fear with the weapons God has given me. These weapons are not carnal. They are mighty weapons!
With these mighty weapons, I break the spirit that will cause me to fight physically. I will win the fight in the name of Jesus.

———◆———

Response 3: Freeze

An alternative response is to remain silent and immobilised when fear assails our minds, hoping that by doing so, fear will disappear. However, this is another deceptive tactic of the enemy. Fear convinces us to stay quiet and keep our struggles hidden. It feeds us lies about potential judgement from people if we speak out. This freezing effect strangles our existence, leading to isolation, social anxiety, and an inability to express ourselves. Being engulfed by fear can create a sense of being frozen in place.

John 10:10 says the enemy only comes to steal, kill and destroy. Whenever fear comes at you, remember that it's an attempt from the enemy to steal from, kill or destroy you. The way out is to rise and boldly confess in the face of fear: *"I will not freeze. Satan will not shut me down. Satan will not oppress or suppress me. The Bible tells me that Jesus came so I may have life to the fullest. I declare that I will run toward God where you can do me no harm. I am a child of God, so you cannot touch me. I will not freeze!"*

Run towards God today. He is offering you the gift of life. He is waiting for you with an open hand. Hurry to Him and engage in a conversation with Him. He holds the gift of life and the gift of a sound mind, and this gift does not include fear.

—◦◦◦◦—

Confession against the spirit of fear:

Right now, I have the spirit of God alive in me. I will not fear. I will not freeze.

The law of the spirit of life in Christ Jesus has set me free from the law of sin and death. I am not under the law of sin and death. I am in Christ Jesus.

—◦◦◦◦—

Response 4: Fawn

This is also a common response to fear, and it entails a compromise to please and protect the very person or thing that causes us to fear. This type of response often occurs in abusive situations. As a survival mechanism, we have an overwhelming desire to keep the abuser happy, hoping that this will keep the abuse at bay, that your ability to keep them sweet is the determining factor of whether the abuse continues. Fawning is a belief system activated by the brain to keep the abused person as safe as possible in a bad situation.

We cannot compromise with fear by enabling it to continue to go unchallenged. God has bestowed upon us the gifts of love and a sound mind. Fear is the absence of love. Yielding to negative situations from a place of fear is evidence that there is an absence of love. As difficult as these situations are, you are better off without them. Do not support wrongdoing; especially wrong against oneself, this is not the life of love God wants for you.

———◦◈◦———

Say this confession:

The Lord is on my side; I will not fear.

*I am a child of God. I will not compromise with evil.
I will not say evil is good.
I will not support what is evil.*

*I carry the light of God.
I will not walk in darkness. I will not be an enabler
of evil in Jesus' name. Amen.*

———◦◈◦———

CHAPTER 2

TYPES OF FEAR

There is an unending list of different types of fear. However, the principles required to break free from any type of fear are the same. While I may not touch on your specific fear or struggle, you can gain freedom by applying the truths stated about overcoming other fears.

Before delving into various types of fear, it is important to clarify a word that can be confusing, which is "respect." Respect is often used in the context of having a reverential fear for someone. For example, the scriptures often use the phrase, "the fear of the Lord." In context, it is used to describe a high form of respect for God. Respect differs from fear; it signifies honour. It is a deep admiration for someone or something due to their abilities, qualities, or achievements, and it is earned through positive actions. If I respect you, I should not be afraid of you. Fear, on the other hand, involves an unpleasant awareness of danger. When we say we fear God, it means we honour and respect Him, not out of fear of His power but for His unconditional love, grace, mercy, protection, and provision.

Dear reader, get ready to walk free from the spirit and intimidation of fear. This chapter will examine the different ways in which fear manifests, include fear of man or failure, even death and sickness. Let us explore how fear can grip a person's life.

FEAR OF MAN

This type of fear is ever with us, but after reading this book and with the help of the Holy Spirit, you will break away from it. In the beginning, God created the heavens, the earth, and all that is in them. After creating man, He instructed them to dominate and rule over everything. While this instruction emphasises man's authority over the created world, it never includes dominion over fellow humans (Genesis 1:26-28).

The moment you are born again, you bear the image of God and carry His DNA. However, in the Garden of Eden, the first man disrupted this union. God had set terms and conditions, but Adam and Eve violated them through sin and disobedience. They disobeyed God, and the consequences were immediate. They became afraid, and fear opened the door for the breakdown in the relationship between God and man.

From this point onward, fear extended beyond sin and disobedience; man began to fear his fellow man due to dangers and insecurities that had become a fabric of society, and the essence of love had gone missing. The fear of man leads to hiding and secrecy (Genesis 1:8). God altered the dynamics at the point of man's disobedience. He told the woman that because of her choice to sin and disobey, her husband would now rule over her.

When I gave my heart and life to Christ, I heaved a sigh of relief because I understood, at that point, that fear no longer had a hold on me. 2 Corinthians 5:17 reveals that once you confess the Lordship of Christ, you become a new creation. Old things have passed away, so you revert to the original intent and purpose of God for your life. Whether you are male or female, both have equal dominance on created things, and every believer is subject to the lordship of Christ but respect and honour one another in love without fear.

Although I understood this newfound freedom in Christ, my life continued to be governed by fear. I grew up in an environment where fathers ruled their household through fear. I watched mothers unable to utter a word when a man spoke. I saw uncles tell women what they could and could not do. I went to a primary school where, if you did not prostrate or kneel to greet a teacher, you received lashes. I grew up being fearful of different types of maltreatment.

During one holiday, my cousin, who was about ten years old, stayed with us. The poor girl was forced to carry a heavy load three times her weight. If she refused to do so, she would be punished with no food. Fearing the consequence, she would bear the heavy burden while weeping in pain and anguish.

The fear of man compels us to do things we would otherwise reject. The fear of unpleasant outcomes often makes us submissive to man. This fear is not godly, as men position themselves almost in god-like positions over you. The fear of man also becomes a form of idolatry. Upon giving your heart to Christ, you embody the image of God. Salvation is not for fear; it is for love, power, and a sound mind. Fear is not synonymous with a sound mind.

A sister once told me a touching story about a chair that was reserved for her father while growing up. She was constantly warned against sitting there but always wondered why. Don't get me wrong. It could be that this chair was reserved as a mark of honour and respect for the father, but it was presented to this sister from a place of fear and dread.

This honour for "the man of the house" was not meant to instil fear. It also didn't mean if anybody sat on the chair, it was "to do or die." One day, this sister decided to sit on the chair. When she did, she found that there was nothing spectacular about the chair. But sadly, the consequences of her decision were harsh because she was severely beaten (for sitting on her own dad's chair!). This scarred her for the rest of her life. It is something that she cannot forget. To instil fear into the heart of a child is torment and abuse.

Parents sometimes withhold love and affection from children to instil fear in them. Husbands can withhold love from their wives, too, for the same reason. And by instilling fear, they command respect from their wives. In the same way, wives can withhold respect towards their husbands to invoke fear in them. Even those in authority always use fear to intimidate and control their subordinates. We see nations wielding fear against one another. Man uses fear to subjugate and display superiority over the weak.

The fear of man is a satanic trick to bring about chaos and disruption. It can cripple your gut and kill the purpose of God for your life. It compels submission to what you know is wrong. It damages your conscience and diminishes your self-worth. You have the choice to discard fear or frame it on your front door. Liberate yourself from this oppressive spirit; cast it out in the name of Jesus.

Some women have died because of the fear their husbands put upon them. They were not able to speak out concerning the danger they were in until they died. I am also sure that the same applies to men because women can torment men with fear, forcing them to contravene God's will and even theirs.

As a child of God, you have been redeemed from the curse of male dominance and control. Salvation restores you to the true image of God. You are no longer under the yoke. I know of couples, where regardless of the setting, the men always dominate conversations wherever they go while the women keep quiet. Even when the women try to speak, the husbands make it seem as though their wives are only meant to be seen and not heard like a shadow. That is not respect, that is fear, you are a human being, you have a part to play here on earth, you did not just exist to occupy a space, you are not a non-living thing, even if you were a tree, trees move and respond to their environment. You must be relevant in your environment, and to your generation, and your voice must be heard. You are a child of God with a voice and that voice must be heard. Do not allow fear to cripple you and take you out.

In this new generation, we have a rise of new waves bringing up further issues of fear that the previous generations probably never encountered. People are now afraid of how they look, the watchful eyes of others, and the opinions circulating about them. Social media, in particular, has become a breeding ground for fear to infiltrate the lives of our youth. Simple acts like dressing up for an outing become sources of anxiety as they worry about people's perceptions. Some even resort to drugs and alcohol as coping mechanisms, but they end up falling into the devil's traps, thus creating additional forms of baggage for themselves.

Some are even afraid of saying "No" without guilt; they say "Yes" when they do not mean it. Consequently, they become soft targets in the clutches of wrong influences. Joshua 1:9 encourages us to be bold and strong because the Lord is with us. Jesus promised a full life. This kind of life is complete and abundant in Christ. Fear robs us, but love fills us. Material possessions, purchased in an attempt to cover up like Adam and Eve and escape the fear of man, will only bring temporary relief. God did not send His son to earth to condemn us. Instead, He came to liberate us from every form of fear.

Prayer for freedom from the fear of man:

I come against the fear of man and every spirit that causes me to fear my fellow man. Any spirit that causes me to feel intimidated or small has no right to operate in my life anymore. I will hold my head high and stand tall. I will not fear for God is with me, and if God is for me, who can be against me? Nobody!

FEAR OF FAILURE

The fear of failure can be a powerful force that throws us off balance. The devil uses it to keep us from moving forward. Being afraid of failure sometimes makes us put things off and avoid anything that might not be successful. It throws us backwards and makes us afraid to try, to take risks, or even to start new things. Because of this fear, we procrastinate, pushing things forward and delaying what needs to be done. It even makes us afraid of growth.

This fear makes us miss golden opportunities. While avoidance might feel like a temporary escape, we forget that God, through the Holy Spirit, has given us a sound mind that can permanently overcome this fear. My children always tell me to confront my fears by first identifying them and understanding their source. Then, we can look for solutions rooted in Christ's teachings and words.

I know brilliant people who are afraid to go to university simply because they are afraid of failure. They never even try, never giving themselves a chance to succeed. I call this fear of failure the spirit of laziness and lethargy. Our environment has conditioned us to believe that failure is bad. When we fail, we feel ashamed, embarrassed, and like we've disappointed ourselves and others. But, in reality, failure doesn't diminish our worth. For example, as a student, I avoided Maths because I felt I would get a low grade. This did not mean I was worthless; it just meant that I had not developed strong skills in that subject. My worth remains intact to date, and I can still excel in other areas. With this knowledge, I can push through the fear of failure by continuing to learn and grow.

People often view failure as the end of their world, and a tool the devil uses to hinder progress. Instead, we should see it as a learning process and a stepping stone to new experiences and personal development. Remember, as Paul wrote in Philippians 4:13, *"I can do all things through Christ who strengthens me."* When faced with failure, keep trying until you succeed. That's the spirit that conquers the fear of failure.

But remember, fear itself is a spirit. The fear of failure interferes with your destiny, future, and God's plan for your life. However, God's promises in His word grant you the ability to overcome and not fail. As I mentioned earlier, failure isn't the end; it's an opportunity to see things differently and to view the future brighter with the knowledge you've gained.

Fear of failure can stem from a fixed mindset, a belief that "what will be, will be" and nothing can change. This isn't true. You can develop, change, and grow. Your life can improve. Yes, you've made mistakes and failed, but you are not defined by them. We can learn from our mistakes and become better individuals. Your mind might tell you that you'll fail, so why even try? But as a child of God, you possess a growth mindset, a sound mind that can develop and improve with time and experience. Rise, child of God! The Holy Spirit can help you break the fear of failure. Always remember that failure is a learning curve on the path to success.

Here is a list of some people who failed before they found success:

1. *Isaac Newton (1643-1727):* He was a school dropout. He failed and failed again but later became a professor in maths. He formulated the laws of motion and universal gravity. He did not allow his past failure to stop him.

2. *Abraham Lincoln (1809-1865):* Until age 21, he worked on his father's farm. At age 23, he contested the election at the National Assembly, but he failed. He went into the retail business and failed yet again. He began to teach himself law to be admitted into the bar, and then he ran for political

office and succeeded. He became the 16th U.S. president.

3.   *Charles Darwin (1809 – 1882):* He failed as a doctor. His passion for the origin of species led him to the study of the theory of evolution. He thought lectures were boring. He did not like the sight of blood, but he became top-notch in the study of evolution.

4.   *Louisa May Alcott (1832 – 1888):* From the age of 15, she had to take up a job to support her sisters, working as a seamstress. Life was so hard that she contemplated suicide. Being very good at reading and writing, one of her write-ups was published with considerable success. She took a political post and wrote letters for young women; this brought her tremendous fame.

5.   *The Wright Brothers (Orville 1871-1948):* The Wright brothers saw a world of possibility in the way birds, kites, and even balloons fly in the sky. They set their sights on achieving sustained flight in the air. Despite numerous failures and setbacks, they persevered. Today, thanks to their unwavering persistence, we can board aeroplanes and travel comfortably

for hours on this piece of metal in the air. These very machines were crafted by the brothers, who refused to give up on their dream despite repeated failure.

6. *Winston Churchill (1872-1965):* He was the most famous British prime minister in history. He came from a privileged clan, so it was easy for him to enter into the political arena, and within ten years, he was Home Secretary. He later failed in his career and lost his seat after two years. He regained strength and became Chancellor of the Exchequer. He was later kicked out of office but was recalled to become the Prime Minister of Britain. He led Britain to victory and became one of the most celebrated prime ministers of all time.

7. *Walt Disney (1902-1966):* He experienced rounds of failure and became so poor that he began to eat dog food. His first studio 'Laugh-O-Gram which lasted for two years led him to bankruptcy. He made a cartoon 'Oswald the Rabbit' but his managers robbed him off by pushing him to negotiate a low fee or quit. He refused and failed yet again, but he made another character which led to Disney and Mickey Mouse.

8. *JK Rowling (1965):* She was a poor, unemployed, single mother with acute depression. She wrote a script for Harry Potter and the Philosopher's Stone, but publishers refused to print it. When one publisher accepted to publish, she was told the book would not give her any earnings but the rest is history today because over 100 million of the book has been sold, making her a millionaire of her time.

9. *Lady Gaga (1986):* She came from a wealthy home but was always in trouble as she was bullied at school. She had musical talents, but nobody seemed to like her. She would be hired and dropped off after three months. Her first album, The Fame, became number one in the chart and that flipped the coin over for her success.

10. *Benjamin Franklin:* He was the founding father of bifocals and the lightning rod. He dropped out of elementary school because his parents could not afford to send him to school. At ten years old, he read books like crazy, taking every opportune step he could to learn. Today, his name is in the book of those who broke records.

11. *Thomas Edison:* He failed a thousand times but later succeeded in inventing the light bulb you have in your house today.

All of these people and many more did not bow to fear. And like you, they only have one head. What made the difference is that they refused to quit. The trademark 7up was adopted for the carbonated drink because the owner failed six times but succeeded the seventh time. Regardless of how many times you have failed, you can still enjoy the fruits of success. The important thing is to never allow fear of failure to cripple you. You should rather learn from it and try again. The Bible is full of numerous promises that give you rights and opportunities to overcome failure.

Say this confession aloud:

In the name of Jesus, I will not allow fear of failure or my past to stop me from moving forward.

I am a winner. I am an overcomer. I will move forward. Even when I fall, I will get back up and continue to walk without looking back.

I break the hold, power, and chain of the fear of failure holding me back in the name of Jesus.

God will neither leave me nor forsake me. He is
with me always. Even when I am afraid, He tells
me, 'Fear not.' Even if I fail, I will succeed by His
grace. Amen

———◈———

FEAR OF SICKNESS

This is a state of being worried that you may
fall sick, maybe amplified due to past trauma,
the loss of a loved one, or a family pattern of
illness. You have no symptoms, yet fear grips
your mind and affects your body. Sometimes,
a little sensation or minor discomfort releases
in you a fear of severe sickness. At times, you
go on and on checking yourself for possible
signs of sickness. This attitude is not from a
sound mind but from fear.

From a very tender age, even while we are
still in the womb, the fear and thought of sickness lingers around us. We must continually
remind ourselves that fear is not a gift from
God. You can teach your children the effect of
temperature changes instead of teaching them
how they could fall ill if they don't wear their
coats. Teach your child not to be afraid of sickness because Jesus bore our sicknesses and
diseases. When the Bible says we shall not fear

the terror, pestilence, and arrow that fly around, these could be likened to sicknesses and infirmities. Acts 10:38 reveals how God anointed Jesus who went about doing good and healing those who were oppressed.

This is God's promise to us over sickness – healing. Before we get sick, God has already provided a healer. And now, we can live above the fear of sickness, having known that Jesus bore our sicknesses and carried our diseases, and we are healed by his stripes.

A man of God once said, "What you are afraid of will not happen." I believe him, and every Christian ought to think this way, too. But we don't. When we have a headache or a cough, we think of the worst, possible outcome.

Knowing or hearing about people who are sick can also trigger fear of sickness in us. We sometimes think because our cough sounds like that of the person we know, maybe we are sick too. People will start saying to one another, 'Please, what were your symptoms so I can know if the way I am feeling suggests the same?' This is fear talking! That you have the same symptoms does not mean you will suffer the same fate.

Don't get me wrong. I understand that illness sparks up fear, worries and anxiety, but what can our fear do? I used to worry and fear a lot. I would go to the mirror to check my body to see if I was okay. I did this repeatedly until the day the Holy Spirit spoke into my spirit and asked me to sit down. As I did, He requested me to bring a pen and paper. He then instructed me to write down all the solutions and positive results I have attained from fear. I looked up and down but could not account for one positive result. I felt silly and put my head down in shame. He then told me to turn to the other side of the sheet and write truthfully about the negative results fear of sickness had brought to my life.

By the time I began to write down worry, headache, depression, anger, frustration, unforgiveness, temper, and outbursts, amongst others, the paper had almost filled up. Then the Holy Spirit said, "Look at all of these and much more that you will write if I allow you to continue. None of them comes from me but from a fallen place. The fears that you accepted and welcomed birthed all these in you." After that encounter, I decided that what God cannot do for me would remain undone. I decided to begin trusting completely in Him.

The devil plants the fear of sickness in humans to torment and destroy us. And in the same way you can reject a gift you don't want, you can also reject this "gift" of fear. Also, the fear of sickness is a spirit that does not come from God, and if it is not from God, it means it is from the devil. When it comes to dealing with the devil, God gave us the authority to bind the devil and cast it out of our minds. Therefore, when the fear of sickness attacks your mind, you bind the thought and cast it out in the name of Jesus.

Many of us find it difficult to reconcile science with the word of God. The explosion of scientific knowledge, as prophesied in scripture, covers the earth like water. Indeed, science is at its peak, considering that artificial intelligence is now challenging human thought processes more than ever. Yet, as scripture reminds us, we are created in God's image, and "whose report will you believe?" the Bible asks. We choose to believe the Lord's report.

However, as humans, we easily forget this truth amidst the innovations of scientific knowledge. While I respect and admire the ingenuity of human intelligence, I must remember that these are gifts from God. Science itself is not almighty; only God is sovereign.

When fear of sickness grips me, I must strengthen my faith in God's omnipotence and cast aside any doubt. This does not imply that I will not see a doctor if the situation calls for it, but even while doing that, I will bask in the knowledge that the sickness has no hold on me. Remember that fear is often false evidence appearing real. The fear of sickness may seem real, but it becomes reality only when we entertain it. We can combat this fear with the unfailing word of God.

We often unknowingly transfer the fear of sickness to our children at a young age. Simple phrases like "put on your coat or you'll catch a cold" can instil the fear of cold weather and illness. Instead, we should educate them about the world around them. This will empower them to make informed decisions.

We often speak fear induced words without realising it. However, Psalm 118:6 reminds us, *"The Lord is on my side; I will not fear."* When God speaks, He provides the power to fulfil His word. If He says, "fear not," He equips us to overcome fear. This empowers us to live above the fear of sickness. Shake off this fear and walk in the newness of life found in Christ Jesus.

Here are some powerful promises from God's word that can empower us to overcome fear:

"Fear not, for I am with you; be not dismayed, for I am your God; I will strengthen you, Yes, I will help you, I will uphold you with my righteous right hand."

Isaiah 41:10 NKJV

"Be strong and courageous. Do not be afraid or terrified, because the Lord your God is with you wherever you go."

Deuteronomy 31:6

"Now may the Lord of peace Himself give you peace always and in every way. The Lord be with you all."

2 Thessalonians 3:16 NKJV

Jesus, in Luke 8:50, said we should not be afraid and just believe.

━━━⟐⟐⟐━━━

Say the following with faith:

The lord is on my side I will not fear.

Fear of sickness, I release your grip over me, and I cast you out in the name of Jesus.

Spirit of fear of sickness, you are not from God. Therefore, I reject you; get off me now in the name of Jesus. Amen.

━━━⟐⟐⟐━━━

FEAR OF DEATH

Jesus' death and resurrection annihilated the power of death over us. He gained victory over death on the cross of Calvary and broke the power of death over every believer. His resurrection signifies our elevation with Him. In descending to hell, He seized the keys of death, freeing deceased believers. Through His death, He took away our sins, and disempowered the devil, who held the power of death.

The fear of death arises from sin, as evidenced by God's warning in the Garden of Eden. When our first parents sinned, death entered, and fear ensued. In Ecclesiastes, Solomon emphasises the inevitability of death, highlighting the existence of times and seasons governing the earth, including a time to be born and a time to die. This understanding, however, is sometimes overlooked, leading some to wake up each morning with an intense fear of death.

The fear of death is not a gift from God. In his words to Timothy, Paul affirmed that God has given us the spirit of a sound mind, not the spirit of fear. So, when we fear death, it is considered a disorder, an unsound state of mind.

Having personally faced this kind of fear in the past, especially after losing two younger siblings within a short period, I understand the intense nature of this battle. The fear would sometimes speak loudly, and I would think I would be the next to go. In my dreams, I would see caskets with no occupants. I sought solace from my pastor, who would often pray for me after such episodes. But I later realised this fear was fuelled by the *false evidence appearing real* in my soul realm.

My fear originated from the loss of dear ones, and the devil exploited this vulnerability. As I reflected on my purpose on earth, I understood that when that purpose is fulfilled, I will return to my Maker. I consoled myself with the fact that my siblings died because they had also completed their God-given task on earth. This empowered me to combat the fear with God's word.

Your situation may be different. Various experiences may contribute to the fear of death – witnessing the loss of loved ones, surviving accidents, or enduring bouts of misfortune. Depression and isolation can also open the door to fear.

Romans 12:1-2 instructs believers to present their bodies, which includes their minds, as a living sacrifice to God. This presentation is a responsibility placed on us; we must renew our minds daily. This renewal involves renovating, reconstructing, replacing, rewiring, and regenerating our thoughts. We need to delete and replace what should not be there with what is good and godly. Transforming our minds means removing the fear of death and replacing it with the spirit of a sound mind, the life-giving spirit of God, ensuring that we will live and not die.

Jesus reassured us not to fear those who can touch our bodies but cannot touch our souls. In the contemporary global environment, especially with the influence of social media, young people encounter various fears. Daily exposure to news can bombard them with thoughts of death, including issues such as overdosing, suicidal thoughts, and murder. The fear of death becomes a constant presence in their lives.

Jesus advised against worrying about material needs. He assured us that our Heavenly Father cares for us even more than earthly fathers who give good gifts. Fear is a prison. If you find yourself in a self-imposed prison, let faith rise within you, take back the key, unlock the door, and be set free!

When I lost my sister, the mourning seemed

endless. I fervently prayed and fasted, questioning why my sister, a believer in Christ, had to die so young in a fatal accident. In a dream, the Lord showed me His palm with the nail imprint and also questioned why He had to die at the tender age of 33. When I woke up, I was amazed to find my tears dried, the pain gone, the heaviness lifted, and the fear of death vanished.

What I learnt was that age is not evidence of our assignment. Jesus finished his assignment at age 33, so what is important is not at what age we die but dying without finishing our assignment. Jesus stressed the importance of completing our assignment and finishing well. My prayer for you and me is that we die empty, upon fulfilling the purpose for which we came. While not all deaths or accidents are necessarily God's plan, we trust that being in Him and from Him, He knows and sees all things. In the face of uncertainties, He instructs us not to fear.

Although the devil may have the power to harm our flesh, Jesus encourages us to fear God, who has authority over both our flesh and spirit. Our strength lies in recognising that God has power over death. Therefore, we can rewire our thoughts, minds, and emotions, boldly declaring that death has no dominion over us. Affirming our declaration with confidence, we can live to declare the works of God in the land of the living. No weapon formed against us shall prosper, and we have the authority to condemn and silence any voice instigating the spirit of fear of death in our thoughts. In the name of Jesus, we bind and break free from the chains of fear.

Solomon wisely stated that there is a time to be born and a time to die. Just as the day of our birth is unknown to us, the day of our death might also be unknown unless God reveals it by His grace. Birth is a certainty, and death is inevitable, but what matters most is how we live our lives between these two points.

The fear of death can distract us from the significance of the time we have on earth. What's crucial is what we do with our lives while we are alive, which includes fulfilling our divine destiny, and being useful to ourselves, our families, communities, and the world. Fearing death can potentially lead to a premature death.

God charges us to rise and confront our fear. He has given us the weapons to fight, described as mighty through Him. Confront the root cause of your fear of death boldly. Attack it with the Word of God, declaring, "I shall not die; I will live." Renew your mind, change your thought patterns, and focus on living life to the fullest.

By resisting the devil of the fear of death and aligning with God's plan, we can overcome. Resist, and the devil will flee. It can work for you, just as it has for me. The resurrection of Christ, as documented in Romans 6:9, signifies His victory over death, and if you are in Him, death holds no power over you. While Adam's sin brought death and condemnation, Jesus' death and resurrection severed us from the fear of death. As you apply the truths written in this book, you will move toward liberty and experience true freedom to the fullest.

Say this confession:

I break the hold of the spirit of the fear of death over my life in Jesus' name.

FEAR OF ANIMALS

The fear of animals is another powerful tool used by the devil to cripple individuals. I spent my early years in the city, where there were no electricity failures, bush tracks, or dark areas, as every street and home was well-lit.

However, circumstances changed, and my family moved to a village. My world came to a halt, as we had to live in a thatched house without electricity, surrounded by bush tracks. We shared rooms with rodents, cockroaches, and occasional snakes. This drastic shift felt like living in hellfire. I developed a deep fear of snakes, rats, mice, and dogs, while cockroaches were the only creatures I could tolerate because I could easily kill them. The fear extended to darkness as well.

It was so bad that just the thought of these creatures consumed me. My eyes would constantly scan for them, and quite often, I would spot something. We used to fetch water from the stream, and as soon as I entertained fear, the first thing I would see was a snake. If I imagined a dog biting me, and before I could say, Jack, a dog would come out from nowhere. My fears manifested themselves as I encountered the very things I feared. This fear continued to affect me, and when walking home at night, I would always look back to check who was behind me.

Ironically, I never knew a dog would 'help' my daughter later in life. When she went away to the university, and it was the first time that she had been away from home, she became so scared and lonely that she went into depression. A course mate then advised her to get a pet dog to keep her company, which she did. This dog helped her deal with her fear of dogs.

When she was to return home at some point, she desired to come home with her dog. At first, I froze at the thought that a dog was coming near my home. Two weeks after the poor little thing arrived, I fell in love with the very animal that used to scare the living daylights out of me. And it never bit me as I feared when I was a child. Today, I am free from the fear of animals, and I will not trade my dog for a million dollars!

I also knew a young person who was afraid of spiders. I have even seen children who are afraid of moving dry leaves. Fear is a bondage we are no longer subject to. We are free and must walk in freedom.

The current trend that is oppressing our young ones today is anxiety. It makes them feel timid, telling them they are worthless, ugly, don't meet the requirements, fat, skinny, tall, short, not intelligent, and that no one likes them. The enemy goes further by lying to them that engaging in certain behaviours like taking drugs, smoking, becoming rebellious, getting tattoos all over their bodies, enhancing their physical features, etc., will make them meet societal standards. The list is unending, and the pressure on our young ones is over-whelming. Fear makes many of them stay behind closed doors while leading others into deep depression.

You are not alone; I share your pain. I have been there when demons whispered worth-lessness into my mind. But today, I bring good news: you can come out of that bondage. I did, and today I can write this book.

You can break free; you are not anyone's piece of wood to fumble and mess around with. You are a child of God. You do not have to settle for people's opinions. All those suggestions from the devil are nothing but temporary remedies. The suggestions he gives are lies because he is a liar and the father of all liars. You cannot trust a lie. Jesus is the permanent solution that completely liberates you from the bondage of fear and anxiety.

1 John 3:8 says, *"For this purpose the Son of God was manifested, that He might destroy the works of the devil."* Every single one of our fears can be broken. Henceforth, you can affirm that no type of fear has dominion over you. You can reject, break, stop, and finally destroy any root of fear that comes to terrorise your life in Jesus' name.

He has authorised us to use His name, so use that name to thwart fear. Jesus said, "In my name, you can cast out all devils, and nothing shall by any means hurt you." Through the name of Jesus, victory over fear is guaranteed for you and me.

CHAPTER 3

HOW DOES FEAR ATTACH ITSELF TO US?

We have examined various signs, symptoms, and types of fears that can affect and attack the destiny of a child of God. In this chapter, we will explore the different ways that fear gains access to the life of a believer. Proverbs 26:2b states that a *"curse causeless shall not come"* (KJV). This means that nothing happens without a cause. But first, we have to mark a distinction between a *believer* and an *unbeliever*.

Believer

The word *believer*, in a Christian context, means a person who believes in the lordship of Jesus Christ, and having confessed verbally, believes in their heart that Jesus Christ is the Lord and Saviour of the world. To be a believer is to also believe in the death and resurrection of Christ that He died and rose on the third day. When a confession of faith is sincerely made from the heart, then you are referred to as a born-again believer in Christ Jesus

Unbeliever

This second group of people were also created by God, but they are yet to come to the faith as the believer has done. They have not yet confessed the lordship of Jesus Christ. They may also have rejected this confession and decided never to confess Jesus Christ as their Lord and Saviour. They are not to be judged or condemned by anyone, because Jesus died for all (both believers and unbelievers). God gave each of us the will to make choices. At times, an unbeliever may enter the realm of knowledge and experience a change of heart, confessing Christ as their Lord and Saviour. On the other hand, a believer may equally drift away from faith and become an unbelieving believer.

As believers, sin no longer has dominion over us. However, if a believer, especially someone new to Christianity, is ignorant of the knowledge of the Word of God, they become vulnerable to the lies of the enemy. The adversary eagerly awaits opportunities to attack their minds and sow confusion. While an unbeliever, created in God's image, may be unfamiliar with the terms used here, believers in Christ should be well-acquainted with them.

I believe that nothing happens without a reason, so in relation to fear, some of the things that often trigger it include sin, ignorance, and curses. There are many other triggers, but we shall examine these three major ones.

SIN

Sin is defined as an offence against a moral law. It can also be defined as a moral evil committed deliberately to violate the will of God. Sin is an offence against God, who He is and what He represents.

Sin originated from the first man, Adam, who despised God's instructions and ate the fruit God told him not to eat. By disobeying God, the consequence was that sin entered his bloodline, transmitted to all the descendants of humankind – including you and me.

When we sin against God, it goes beyond offending Him. We also harm one another. Our sin affects not only God but also ourselves. For instance, when you take what does not belong to you, in addition to disobeying God's will, you deprive the rightful owner of their property. Let's say I stole money intended for your children's school fees. There is no doubt that I have sinned against God. But I have also caused you pain and denied your children access to education. This is how the cycle of sin affects various aspects of our lives.

So, when we sin, we break our relationship with God and others. When this happens, we break the hedge of protection around us, thus opening access for evil spiritual attacks. For a believer, the word of God gives us protection over sin because when we give our lives to Christ, the power of sin and death is broken over our lives. The Bible, 2 Corinthians 5:21, says, *"For God made Him (Jesus) who knew no sin to be sin for us, that we might become the right-eousness of God in Him."*

Sin gives access to the spirit of fear, but that door can be closed against Satan by the righteousness of God in Christ Jesus. Sin gives access to the devil to come in and dwell in our lives. It breeds and feeds fear in our minds and causes us to live a life of fear. It also separates us from God and makes us doubt our standing with him.

When God came into the Garden of Eden to have fellowship with Adam and Eve, and He could not find them in His presence, He called out to them. And Adam replied, "We are hiding because we are afraid." What made Adam and Eve afraid was the sin of disobedience.

TIPS TO BREAKING THE POWER OF FEAR CAUSED BY SIN

1. Be a student of the Bible and study the word of God on a constant and persistent basis, so that His word becomes deeply rooted in your heart. This will transform your nature and character to be like Christ.

2. Strive to live a holy life that is pleasing to God.

3. Strive to abide in His presence.

4. Pray in season and out of season.

5. Hang around people of like minds. Evil association corrupts good, and you become like those you mix with.

6. Desire and hunger for God through fellowship with the brethren, prayer, fasting and love and passion for His word.

7. Be conscious of sin.

8. Meditate to transform your mind to the will of God.

9. Flee every appearance of sin. Fear is a torment, so avoid its lust.

For unbelieving brothers and sisters, there is limited power to engage in spiritual battles. The Bible, which is the believer's manual, reveals that the devil is an 'old serpent' that has been present since the beginning of time. Beating him is beyond our capacity, so we must attach ourselves to the One who can. Without being believers in Christ, we cannot claim the rights He has acquired.

Therefore, unless you are born again, you remain vulnerable to the devices of the evil one, and he remains your master with the power to rule over you. Your own power of protection is insufficient; we need the divine protection of God to engage in the spiritual fight against the enemy.

IGNORANCE

An ignorant person lacks knowledge or awareness. When we say a person is ignorant, sometimes it does not mean that the person does not know something, but it could mean that the person does not have a specific body of learning or learning in the topic or subject area in question.

Dr Myles Munroe (of blessed memory) puts it this way: the greatest enemy of man is not sin or the devil but ignorance. He said that ignorance and the rejection of knowledge is the cause of all destruction. Hosea 4:6 stresses that the people of God are destroyed for lack of knowledge. They have rejected knowledge and have forgotten the laws of God. That verse does not suggest that knowledge is not available rather it suggests a lack of it. Ignorance makes us unaware of how the devil plots against us to destroy the will of God for our lives.

What you know in life is based on what you have learned. A lack of knowledge goes beyond not just having it; it can also refer to having access to knowledge but choosing not to use or apply it. This is the devil's playground; he exploits our lack of knowledge and areas of ignorance to afflict us with fear.

Ignorance can make you learn the wrong things, and you might mistakenly believe they are right. Being an expert in errors is a dangerous situation. Ignorance provides an open door for demons of fear. It also robs us of God's promises for our lives. To discern and combat this spirit, we need a wealth of knowledge from the Word of God, which can dispel ignorance and drive away fear.

Ignorance serves as a breeding ground for error and blindness. It is capable of invading homes, individuals, or entire communities with evil spirits. It is even more perilous for leaders, as their ignorance impacts those under their leadership, be it a church or a family (Matthew 15:14). Leaders who are blind may inadvertently lead their followers into a ditch.

It is crucial not to ignore or trivialise knowledge, especially for leaders, as lack of knowledge provides an opportunity for the devil to infiltrate and disturb our lives. Obtaining true knowledge from the Word of God is essential. Ignorance is not an excuse before God. Hence, the pursuit of godly knowledge and wisdom are strongly advised, as what we do not know has the potential to harm us.

RECOMMENDATIONS FOR BREAKING THE POWER OF FEAR THROUGH IGNORANCE:

1. The remedy for ignorance is the knowledge of God's word. Study and do your best to present yourself to God approved, a workman who has no reason to be ashamed, accurately handling and skilfully teaching the word of truth (2 Timothy 2:15). People often say that knowledge is power, but I have learned that not all knowledge is power. The knowledge of truth found in God is what we need.

2. Create uninterrupted times to seek the face of God. Spend personal time with God in a place of retreat, and endeavour to hear Him speak to you. According to Dr Myles, when you do not know the purpose of a thing, abuse becomes inevitable. In the same manner, the truth can only come through the maker of a thing because he is the only one who knows the product. Moreover, without the manufacturer's manual, one will only be experimenting.

So, the medicine for ignorance is to study the manual page by page until the true light illuminates every dark area. The scripture urges us to let our light shine brightly. You cannot compare the light on your mobile phone with the flood lights in a stadium. Like the latter, shine brightly. Seek knowledge from God's word, and watch ignorance disappear.

Hold fast unto God until He blesses you and frees you from the spirit of ignorance.

CURSES

A curse is an utterance intended to invoke a supernatural power to inflict harm or punishment on someone or something. To say that it is an utterance means that curses are spoken words, incantations, divinations inflicted against a person with the intention of harming them. Curses can flow through a bloodline; in this sense, things that were spoken and conjured in past generations, spiritually and physically, can flow through to new generations unaware of past spiritual entanglements. God put a curse on Cain when he killed his brother Abel; the curse ran through his bloodline.

Curses can make a person, family, community, and even land suffer devastating consequences. These curses can emanate from disobedience to God, to parents, to those who have leadership positions over you. Curses can also be set in motion by the shedding of blood, deprivation, injustice, breaking of covenants and agreements, the worship of idols, evil associations, to name a few. They affect our ability to experience the fullness of the joy of the Lord. When the joy of the Lord is absent in your life, it gives room for fear. When Adam disobeyed God, he lost the realm of blessing and entered the realm of curses. Consequently, death became inevitable. Adam's sin brought a curse on the land. The Bible said he would labour and sweat before the land could yield its fruit to him.

Curses can hand you over to the spirit of fear because when those who are meant to protect you become your enemy, it leaves you vulnerable. And when you are vulnerable, it becomes easier for fear to creep in.

RECOMMENDATION FOR BREAKING THE POWER OF CURSES

1. Jesus reversed the curse. In John 14:6, He said, "I am the way to the truth and the truth that leads to life and that life gives us freedom from the curse of the law." The first step to enjoying this freedom is by surrendering our all to Him. And He will empower you to walk above the curse of the law.

2. When we choose Christ, we choose blessings instead of curses, and blessings are more powerful than curses. The blessings of God over you are greater than the curses of the devil. It is essential to exercise this right and enforce your victory over curses.

3. Accepting the Lordship of Christ will ward off any curse that gives the devil access into our lives. Jesus' death on the cross broke the power of curse over every believer, so as soon as you give your life to Christ, you are redeemed from the curse of the law and the evil one. Even if the enemy tries to attack, you must stand on the victory you have through the redemptive power of the blood.

Use the weapon of your warfare given to you in Christ Jesus. The weapon comprises His name, His blood and His word. They arm you against fear and curses. You can declare the word of God, which is your battle axe, over your life and family.

Jesus is reminding us to rejoice because we have overcome the world, and greater is He who is in us than he who is in the world. We have victory over curses through Jesus Christ. We have nothing to fear or worry about.

———⊲♦⊳———

Say this prayer:

I rejoice the fact that Jesus has overcome the world. The fear that is in the world has been overcome by Him, so it does not have to overwhelm or consume me. Lord, help me hear your voice louder than any other voice, or lie of the enemy.
In Jesus Name, Amen.

———⊲♦⊳———

CHAPTER 4

GOD'S WAY

In Romans 8:2, Apostle Paul established two biblical principles on the two spiritual laws at work in the world. The law of the spirit of life is found in Christ Jesus, and it sets us free from the law of sin and death, the second law that keeps us in bondage.

The word *law*, according to Webster's dictionary, is an established principle which can be depended upon to work in the same way at any time. Examining the laws stated in Romans 8, we see a law of reciprocals just as the North and South are reciprocal. Though they are in opposite directions, they correspond to one another. Faith is God's way but fear is Satan's way. God is the creator of all things, but Satan perverts what God has created for an evil agenda. We see this in the way he perverted God's original plan at creation by deceiving the first man. God gave Adam authority to rule and take charge of everything He created, but Satan, through deception, usurped this authority to govern the spiritual laws of the earth. While God set spiritual laws in motion for life, Satan perverted these laws, thus setting death in motion instead. Death became life perverted; hate became love perverted and fear became faith perverted.

The faith that God gave Adam was meant to sustain him and all generations after him, but when Satan deceived him, that force of faith was perverted, and the spiritual law of fear and death came in to kill and to destroy. Faith produces life but fear has nothing but death to offer. When there is faith at work in your life, you can overcome fear. In the same manner, love will always overcome hate and prosperity overcome poverty.

Note that fear, as a counterfeit, will never be a legal tender, and it will never supersede the original faith and love. You will always find a promise from the Word of God that gives you victory over any deception the devil throws your way.

Adam bowed to Satan by listening and obeying him, and then Satan took over rulership from him. Similarly, when we bow, listen, and obey the spirit of fear that the devil throws into our minds, we set in play the law of sin and death. It is essential to remember that in the beginning, Adam did not know how to die; all he knew was how to live and all he knew was God's word. However, when he went against God's word, he experienced spiritual and physical death. As believers in Jesus Christ, we are blessed that we have been redeemed from the law of sin and death and reconciled back to God through the blood of the everlasting covenant.

Here we can see the laws in motion: if Adam obeyed God, he lived, but when he disobeyed God, death took over, and the law of life changed to the law of death. In the hand of God, it was the law of life, but in the hand of Satan, it was perverted to the law of death. When we come to Christ, we are washed with his blood, and we are required to continue in obedience to Him and His word.

The whole world flows in a negative downfall and destructive streams. It operates under satanic negativity, bad news, negative comments, and destructive rumours. We are surrounded by fear to the point that it has now become our reality. This happens because when we give thoughts, speech, and action to negative forces, we set fear in motion.

Although some people think that a little fear is healthy, I disagree with this notion. I consider it a lie from the pit of hell. There is no such thing as healthy fear; there is no such thing as a combination of God's way and Satan's way. The only true method of operation is this: God's way and God's word.

As the substance of things hoped for and the evidence of things not yet seen with the physical eye, faith is a spiritual force that reaches out into the reality of the things you need in this world. It stretches into the spirit's supply and brings those needs into the physical manifestation. How does this work? Romans 10:17 says, *"Faith cometh by hearing and hearing by the word of God"* (KJV). Meditating on the word and acting on it increases the capacity for faith. The word will then produce love, healing, prosperity, and wisdom in every area of your life.

Your faith is strengthened when it is put into use; it is like a muscle. It must be exercised to be effective. If you tie your right arm to your side and do not use it for several years, you will lose the strength in that arm. Just as faith comes by hearing the word of God, fear comes by hearing the lies of Satan.

A friend of mine in desperate need of prayer once called my mother in the middle of the night. He was in the hospital for surgery, but fear had taken control of him to such an extent that the doctors wouldn't operate on him. Fear attracts sickness and death. My mother went in, prayed for this friend, and cast out the spirit of fear, and he was healed instantly.

Guard your thoughts and discern their truth. This will help you identify whose voice you're hearing and choose which to follow. The voices promoting sin and death belong to Satan, while those offering good and love come from God. But at the end of the day, the final decision rests with you, not the devil or God, because you possess the willpower to make choices. God, in His loving nature, is urging you to choose life. If you haven't done that already, or if you have strayed, I trust that you will ultimately decide to give your heart to Him. He welcomes you back with open arms, for His way is always better. Choose life, choose God's way today, and you will be glad you did.

—⟡—

Say this prayer:

O God, I submit completely to you, my mind and my thoughts. Help me to choose the life of freedom from fear. Help me to discern your voice, and to replace negative voices with the truth of your word.

—⟡—

CHAPTER 5

DEATH VERSUS LIFE

In this chapter, we will explore the significance of Jesus Christ's temptation and his unwavering obedience. Unlike Adam, who succumbed to temptation, Jesus remained sinless. His sinlessness demonstrates his perfect character and it helped in fulfilling his role as the sacrificial lamb for humanity's salvation.

By resisting temptation and embracing his divinely ordained path, Jesus offered humanity the opportunity to overcome sin and death. His obedience serves as a powerful example for us to follow in our own journeys of faith.

The price Jesus paid was twofold:

- He delivered us from the force of fear and death and the bondage it brings.

- He destroyed all the works of the devil over our lives.

> *"Since therefore the children share in flesh and blood, he himself likewise partook of the same things, that through death he might destroy the one who holds the power of death, that is, the devil, and deliver all those who through fear of death were subject to lifelong slavery."*
>
> **Hebrews 2:14-15 ESV**

Through his death and resurrection, Jesus conquered death and Satan, who held the power of death. This victory grants us freedom from the bondage of fear that Satan often uses to control us. As children of God, we are empowered by Jesus' sacrifice to declare our freedom from fear and live boldly in faith.

You may wonder, "How can I know that Jesus did this for me?" My answer is that the written word of God states that Jesus, on the cross of Calvary, took upon Himself and absorbed all the costs of the law, spiritually and physically. He went to hell and took back the keys of authority, releasing first the saints whom the devil held captive. Upon His resurrection, he declared, *"All authority and all power I give to you."* Hebrews 2:14 reveals that Jesus destroyed Satan and allowed us to walk in freedom.

The moment you give your heart to the saving grace of Christ, you will begin to walk and enjoy the blessings of the law of the spirit of life. This is the law that has liberated us from fear. Remember, you have not been given the spirit of bondage to fear. Jesus' coming has broken that bondage. This is why it is crucial to always walk in faith.

Faith will always win over fear. When you apply faith, it flows through your entire being. On the other hand, fear antagonises your being. While faith helps, fear hurts. Satan will do his best to destroy you and your testimony as a believer. After all, his goal is to remove you from your field of action. He uses fear to challenge the promises of God over your life. He tries to make it look as if God's promises would not work for you. He wants to desperately convince you that faith will not work and that Jesus' sacrifice at Calvary was not good enough. He is nothing but the father of all lies. Why should you believe a liar?

Satan cannot touch you if you stand on the word of God. Our faith in God and His word is the upholding in our lives.

> *"And He is the radiance of His glory and the exact representation of His nature and upholds all things by the word of His power. When He had made purification of sins, He sat down at the right hand of the Majesty on high."*
>
> **Hebrews 1:3 BSB**

This verse portrays Jesus as the perfect representation of God. We move and bask in victory over fear through His name.

BASIC CHARACTERISTICS OF FAITH

- Faith is a spiritual force.
- Faith is God's creative power.
- Faith is the substance of things hoped for and the evidence of things not yet seen with the physical eye.
- Faith is an absolute, complete, and perfect dependency on the truth of God's word.

Faith is not produced in your head but in your heart. And this power is generated by the word of God. You get the word into your heart through various means such as hearing the word of God repeatedly, engaging in study, prayer, fasting, praise, worship, and more. Just as you won't get any power from your car by pouring water into the gas tank, your spiritual life gains its power from God's word just as how a car gains power from petrol. If you allow fear to dominate, it will permeate your spirit and hinder the development of the faith required to overcome life's circumstances.

CHAPTER 6

IT'S A LOVE WALK

The Bible, in 1 John 4:18, affirms that perfect love dispels fear. The verse states that *"There is no fear in love; but perfect love casts out fear, because fear involves torment. But he who fears has not been made perfect in love."*

Drawing a parallel with Deuteronomy 28:1-14, it is highlighted that as long as Israel obeyed the commandments of the Lord, they had no reason to fear anything or anyone. Similarly, in the new covenant, believers are commanded to believe in the name of Jesus Christ and love one another (1 John 3:22-24). This illustrates that believers are called to walk in love irrespective of others' actions. Love is the highest walk for every believer, and as God is love, having God in our lives means that the love of God resides in us. When we walk in love, fear has no place, as God is not associated with fear or failure.

When fear creeps in, confront it boldly right on the spot. A minute's delay can allow it to fester. Rebuke it with all your power, using the word of God as your shield. According to Galatians 3:13-14, *"Christ has redeemed us from the curse of the law, having become a curse for us (for it is written, "Cursed is everyone who hangs on a tree), that the blessing of Abraham might come upon the Gentiles in Christ Jesus, that we might receive the promise of the Spirit through faith."* Hebrews 2:15 equally states that God will free those, who, through fear of death, were subject to slavery all their lives.

Embrace faith by meditating on God's promises and purpose for your life. Dwell on positive thoughts. Spend quality time fulfilling your purpose on earth, spend time in prayer, and seek His face to know His plan for your life and pursue it. Trust in God's provision, as Matthew 6:28–31 reminds us. Reject negative thoughts and choose instead to focus on God's promises. This approach empowers you to overcome fear and live a life anchored in faith.

A bird has the right to fly above your head but has no right to lay its eggs on top of your head unless you allow it. In the same manner, though you cannot prevent the devil from throwing thoughts into your mind, you can prevent those thoughts from taking root and germinating, from small seeds to big trees. Resist processing and dwelling on the devil's thoughts. The Bible instructs believers to cast down imagination and every high thing that exalts itself against the knowledge of God, bringing every thought into captivity to the obedience of Christ.

If you allow these thoughts to incubate and become a part of your declarations, they will take root and grow abundantly in your heart. This abundance will continue to produce and yield a harvest. In Matthew 12:35, it is stated, *"The good man brings out of his good treasure what is good, and the evil man brings out of his heart the evil treasure, which is evil"* (LSB). Speaking positive affirmations helps cultivate a good treasure in your heart such that it becomes a stronghold ready for manifestation.

For your faith to take root in your spirit, you will declare the word, believe it, meditate on it, chew it, and put it into practice until you get the desired result. Instead of dwelling on your 'stinking thinking', develop the habit of speaking the word of God over your life in every situation. Stop practising fear; stop entertaining it in your daily conversation. It is not from God; the result is negative.

Love surpasses hate and fear. Jesus underscores the importance of love when He said, "Love one another as I have loved you." Love does not equate foolishness, and it does not mean living without boundaries. God's love calls us to lead a disciplined life, characterised by good conduct and adherence to godly virtues.

When Jesus drove out the merchants from the temple, it was an act of love. Similarly, when God expelled Adam and Eve from the Garden of Eden, it was an act of love. So, do not misunderstand the concept of love so that the devil will not distort its meaning. The love of God comes with boundaries. Therefore, lead a life that aligns with God's will, a love life that pleases Him and stands as the greatest law that the devil cannot overcome or disrupt.

CHAPTER 7

DIVINE PROTECTION

I once had a spectacular experience of God's protection during one of my trips to my home country Nigeria. I wanted to go to a bank in Lagos State to withdraw a huge sum of money to buy a car. I went from Lagos to Benin with two suitcases loaded with money, and I headed to take a local flight to my destination.

In Lagos, the capital of Nigeria back then, there was only one flight to Benin per day. We were all waiting for the plane to land because it had been delayed by three hours. After much frustration, the captain announced that there was no petrol for our flight. Then he recommended that every passenger request a refund. I was stuck! Here I was, at the airport, where I did not know anyone. I had two suitcases filled with money, which made it a high risk to travel by road. Not knowing what to do, I stayed on the tarmac confused and afraid. Around an hour later, a man, who came to the airport to check if there was a flight to the same destination, met me alone stranded on the tarmac.

Suddenly, fear gripped my soul, and I began to tell myself that if anyone knew I was carrying two suitcases filled with money, they would kill me for it. As a young believer, I could only think of one verse to console my fainting heart: 'You cannot bring me this far to leave me.' I kept reciting this over and over in my head. When this man came closer to me, he looked familiar. I then asked him if he was who I thought he was. To my surprise he was the one!

He helped me with my suitcases as we went to the customer service to make inquiries. Suddenly, my heart leapt for joy. At least, I had met a godly man who could help me. On our way to the customer service desk, we heard a lady calling, over the intercom, for the captain of the very flight we were meant to take. She was calling for the captain to fly to Benin because the chairman, who owned the airline, needed to be picked up.

At this point, my newfound friend suggested that we stand close by. The lady asked the captain if he had checked the fuel in the reservoir. He then realised that there was enough fuel to fly to our destination. As the captain boarded the plane, he beckoned to the two of us to board the aircraft. To the glory of God, the plane flew just the two of us to our destination. When he landed, another manager enquired why he had come, and he said he was told to come and pick up the chairman, but the chairman had already taken another plane. God's miracle of protection made all things good even amid our fears. God can provide angelic protection just because of you. He will not bring you this far to leave you in the middle of nowhere. He can't do that because it is not in His nature to do so.

My friend and I were the only passengers on the flight. I saw it as God's provision and protection. Whenever fear rears its ugly head, declare these words: *"I shall not fear the arrows that fly by noonday; He shall preserve my soul. I will not fear because I am the righteousness of God. God will protect us from fear in Jesus' name."*

In my work with the Lord, I encounter couples who disallow their spouses from making friends because they fear that these connections might corrupt their partners. While the Bible acknowledges that evil associations corrupt good character, the primary motivation behind this desire is fear. But perfect love casts out fear. If we love and treat each other as Christ loves the church, we won't operate from a place of fear but trust that the Holy Spirit will guide us through our friendships.

According to Matthew 5:14, *"You are the light of the world. A city set on a hill cannot be hidden."* Who lights a candle and puts it under the table? Nobody! If our deeds are right, we will not be afraid. When you practise love in your home with your spouse and children, fear will not have a room in your life.

When Israel walked in the covenant of God and kept the commandments, they had nothing to fear.

> *"If thou shall hearken diligently unto the voice of the Lord thy God to observe and to do all his commandments, which I command thee this day, the Lord shall cause every enemy of fear that revolts against thee to be smitten before thy face."*
>
> **Deuteronomy 28:1 KJV**

The Bible also states:

> *"But to which of the angels has He ever said, "Sit at My right hand, Until I make Your enemies a footstool for Your feet. Are they not all ministering spirits, sent out to render service for the sake of those who will inherit salvation?"*

Hebrews 1:13-14

You are an heir with Christ. This bestows on you the right to godly protection from fear. You are surrounded by an unseen army of angels. God's ministering spirits are always moving with you. But you cannot enjoy these benefits if you don't walk in love.

When you walk in love, the devil will tempt and try you, but he will not succeed. Walking in hate, in disobedience, opens a door, as seen in the scriptures when Israel disobeyed God, they were oppressed by the devil. Disobedience to God's word opens a door for fear to come in, compromising God's protection. True repentance closes the door, opening angelic assistance and God's protection for a believer. These angelic forces work best on our behalf, ensuring the full armour of God is at work, and our prayer life stays unhindered.

When believers walk in agreement with one another and with a person who has a covenant with Jesus, Jesus Himself will be amid that agreement to ensure His words come to pass. The will of the Almighty God can move people and change things. At this point, God can give people in your place if that is what it takes.

As written in 2 Corinthians 10:4-5, *"The weapons of our warfare are not of the flesh, but divinely powerful for the destruction of fortresses. We are destroying speculations and every lofty thing raised against the knowledge of God, and we are taking every thought captive to the obedience of Christ" (NASB)*. The word of God empowers us to conquer any obstacle on our way. The word salvation in the New Testament has more than one meaning. Though we often use it in the context of being born again, it also means being in sound condition. Being saved puts us back in a sound state.

It also means that you can now start walking in divine health. Regardless of your fears, you can walk in the freedom from that fear. We are heirs of God's deliverance wrought when He raised Jesus Christ from the dead. We are delivered from the authority and powers of darkness, delivered from idols, and all the works of satanic oppression.

Read the following scripture:

> *"Now when the servant of the man of God had risen early and gone out, behold, an army with horses and chariots was circling the city. And his servant said to him, 'Alas, my master! What shall we do?' So, he answered, 'Do not fear, for those who are with us are more than those who are with them. Then Elisha prayed and said, 'O Lord, I pray, open his eyes that he may see.' And the Lord opened the servant's eyes, and he saw; and behold, the mountain was full of horses and chariots of fire all around Elisha."*

2 Kings 6:15-17 WEB

This scripture illustrates the power of faith and God's protection.

Our protection from fear and the challenges of life is guaranteed in God. He purchased you with His precious blood, and you are His army general. The whole state of heaven is on guard for your life. Elisha, as read above, was not afraid because he was in a sound condition. He knew the armies of God were there for his protection because he was a man of covenant and rested in God's promises. He was walking by faith. According to Hebrews 1:7, he loved and obeyed God's word, and God was there for him.

The angels did not suddenly come into existence when the servant saw them with his eyes. The angels and the chariot of fire were there all this time. He simply walked in faith and never lost sight of what he wanted.

Just as Elisha was true to God's commandments, you must be faithful in obedience to God and faith in Him. If you are a husband, God commands you to provide, protect, and honour your family. If you are a wife, God commands you to respect your husband. If you are a child or a slave, God requires you to obey godly principles. When we fail to do these, we are unfaithful. When we become unfaithful to the laws of God, we open doors for the law of sin and death to invade our territory. When we love our brothers and sisters as Christ commanded, we abide in the light. And there is no occasion of stumbling when you are walking in love. You can only stumble in the dark.

PRAYERS

Father, open my eyes to any area of fear in my life. I make the decision now that I will refuse to act in fear or practise it in any way. I believe that your love will flow through me and will help me to handle every situation I am confronted with. I confess now that I am delivered from the law of sin and death. Fear, terror, torment, worry, anxiety, sickness and oppression have no place in me. I am a child of the living God. Jesus Christ of Nazareth died in my place so that the power of fear will not abide in me.

I will keep the commandment of God's love and do those things that are pleasing in His sight, with the help of the Holy Spirit residing in me, in Jesus Christ's name. Amen.

I am protected by the ministering angels of God. Keep me in all my ways in Jesus' name.

Because the love of God is made manifest in me, I walk free from fear, intimidation, rejection, and discouragement in the name of Jesu. This is the beginning of the highest quality life that I will ever have or know.

PRAYER OF SALVATION

If you want to make peace with God, say the following prayer:

"Heavenly Father, I come to you in the name of Jesus. Your word says in Acts 2:21 that it shall be that everyone who calls on the name of the Lord will be saved. I am calling on you now. I pray and ask Jesus to come into my heart and to be Lord over my life. Romans 10:9-10 also mentions that "If thou shalt confess with thy mouth the Lord Jesus and shall believe in thy heart that God raised him from the dead, thou shall be saved. For with the heart, one believes unto righteousness and with the mouth confession is made unto salvation." Right now, I confess that Jesus is Lord and I believe in my heart that God raised him from the dead. I receive you, Lord. Jesus Christ, come into my heart." Amen.

If you made that confession from your heart, you are now a child of God. Welcome into the kingdom! Hallelujah! You are now a new creation. God has generated a brand-new spirit within you, which has the power to defeat the sinful nature in you!

Now look for a Bible-believing church, where you will become a member to increase your faith as a believer.

Write or email us (details are at the end of

the book), and we will send you materials to assist you in your Christian walk. You are no longer a slave to fear because you are from now on a child of God.

PRAYER FOR THE INFILLING OF THE HOLY SPIRIT

Matthew 7:11 says, *"If ye again being evil know how to give good gifts unto your children, how much more shall your heavenly Father give the Holy Spirit to them that ask him?"* (KJV). This quote highlights God's willingness to provide good gifts, including the Holy Spirit, to those who ask.

If you desire to be filled with the Holy Spirit, say this prayer:

I fully expect to speak in other tongues as the Holy Spirit gives me utterance. I confess that Jesus is Lord, and I believe in my heart that God raised him from the dead. I am saved; I am delivered. I am a born again, spirit-filled believer. I will never be the same again. I am connected to God's heavenly kingdom. All the days of my life, I will worship continually praising my God now unto eternity in Jesus' name. Amen.

CHAPTER 8

DON'T GIVE UP THE FIGHT

The more you meditate on fear, the more it grows in your life. It will make you utter things that have not happened as though they already have. You must stand up and fight against the spirit of fear. Do not give up the fight. Fight back with the weapon God gave you. You do not have to act in fear. You must be bold enough to say 'No' when the answer is 'No' without fear or favour. Give fear no place in your life. Resist it with all your might. The word resist here means to be firm, to be resolute, to stampede, to stand against, and to fight against it. Let boldness rise within you to stand and fight against it. If you sense it rising within you, stop wherever you are and take authority over it.

> *"Now in the fourth watch of the night Jesus went to them, walking on the sea. And when the disciples saw Him walking on the sea, they were troubled, saying, "It is a ghost!" And they cried out for fear. But immediately Jesus spoke to them, saying, "Be of good cheer! It is I; do not be afraid." And Peter answered, "Lord, if it is You, command me to come to You on the water." So He said, "Come." And when Peter had come down out of the boat, he walked on the water to go to Jesus. But when he saw that the wind was boisterous, he was afraid; and beginning to sink, he cried out, "Lord, save me!"*

Matthew 14:25-27

This passage is an excellent example of faith versus fear. Jesus was walking on the water and Peter asked if he could join him to which Jesus replied, "come". Peter heard the word 'come' and he acted on it. He stepped out of the boat and started walking towards Jesus. However, when he saw the mighty wind, fear creeped into his mind within that moment, and he began to sink. Fear made him sink.

When he first stepped out of the boat, he was acting in faith, but fear came over him and dominated his entire being, thus causing his faith to fail.

If Peter had rebuked the wind, it would have ceased, but he failed to do this. Instead, he gave in to fear and the result was defeat. Fear fights faith; it always strives to make the words of God fail. The onus lies on you to resist fear with faith. Jesus said, *"Truly I say to you, whoever says to this mountain, 'Be taken up and cast into the sea,' and does not doubt in his heart, but believes that what he says is going to happen, will grant him. Therefore, I say to you, all things for which you pray and ask, believe that you have received them, and they will be granted to you"* (Mark 11:23-24 NASB).

When you speak to a mountain by faith, you put the invisible force of God's creative power into action. When faith-filled words come out of your mouth, they are backed by the spirit of God and the angels of God will carry out your request to move mountains. You are the only one who can withdraw that power with your thoughts. You are the only one who can destroy fear.

One day, the Holy Spirit dropped some words in my heart. He said, "You are very knowledgeable, and you know when someone is lying to you, yet you choose to believe them." I reflected on that for some time and realised that the devil is the father of all lies, so when he speaks, we should recognise his words as lies.

Though he cannot force you, his lies can convince you and make you believe he is telling you the truth. A person of faith will meditate on God's words instead of worrying and, with the force of the word of God, will tell the mountain, "Be thou removed and be thou cast into the sea." After you have spoken the word of faith, the next step is to support the words by praising God until the mountain becomes a plain. While this may not be as easy as it appears, you must understand that nothing good comes easy. You do not win a battle by lying down; you win by not giving up in the fight. You must fight till you win. A famous music artist, Bob Marley, once said, "He who fights and runs away will live to fight another day".

A church member once said to me: "Since I gave my heart to Christ, it seems the battle is more than before." Perhaps you feel the same way. Before you gave your life to Christ, the battle was not raging then because you were already a captive. The devil fought the battle over your soul and captured you into his kingdom. Why will he fight again for your soul when he already has you? But now, you have escaped through the blood of Jesus. You are free from his captivity, so the only thing he can do to fight your liberty in Christ is to throw lies to frustrate your journey and make it hard for you to enjoy your God-given life. The word of God in 1 Peter 5:8-9 says, *"Be of sober spirit, be on the alert. Your adversary, the devil, prowls around like a roaring lion, seeking someone to devour. But resist him, firm in your faith, knowing that the same experiences of suffering are being accomplished by your brethren who are in the world" (NASB).*

In this scripture, we are instructed to resist and fight against the enemy. These words are the action words of a fighting soldier. You don't fight lying down; you fight to enforce the victory already won for you. When He was on the cross, Jesus said, "It is finished." Rise and fight the enemy to give back all your stolen goods – your peace, joy, deliverance, money, and children.

Faith is activated when we articulate, demand, and command things as though they already exist. Let us assert and reclaim all the precious promises God bestowed upon us at creation. He said in Genesis, "Let us make man in our image and our likeness and let them have dominion." Dominion implies being in charge of what rightfully belongs to you. If you need something, and though you have not physically received it, believe in your heart that it is available for you. By doing so, you align with God's plan for you, and you will receive that promise from your faithful Father.

Matthew 12:34 states, *"You brood of vipers, how can you, being evil, speak what is good? For the mouth speaks out of that which fills the heart."* This verse suggests that whatever we store up in our soul, what is pressed down or accumulated inside us, will eventually be revealed when we speak. If fear fills our hearts, our words will reflect that fear. And if faith fills us, the promises of God and words of faith will flow out. Both fear and faith have corresponding harvests, either negative or positive.

What do your utterances communicate? Is it fear or faith? What kind of harvest do you desire as well? Death or life? Make a conscious decision to change your confession now and speak in faith. Alter the thoughts in your heart because from the heart, both good and evil emerge. Start speaking and thinking about the things you want to see manifest in your life and destiny. God is watching over you, ready to fulfil the good desires of your heart. He is not merely a God with good things to give you; He is inherently good and intends to do you good, not harm. Whatever fills your heart abundantly will inevitably come out of your mouth. Your spirit is either filled with faith or fear, love or hate, and your confession serves as the best gauge.

Are you engaged in the good fight of faith? Life operates on the principle of seedtime and harvest time. As stated in Genesis 8:22, *"While the earth remains, Seedtime and harvest, cold and heat, winter and summer, and day and night shall not cease."* Fear itself is a seed that we must not allow to germinate. The enemy may roar like a lion, but he is not the true lion. Jesus Christ is the Lion of Judah. Know your divine heritage, and embrace the victory you have through Christ. Fear is like sowing the wrong seeds, but it brings nothing but loss. However, faith will give you profit. Enter into that territory of faith and receive God's promises. You are not fighting to obtain it; rather, you are fighting to enforce the victory that is already yours in Christ Jesus.

Do not compromise your faith with fear. Do not allow any person to tell you it is not possible. If God says it is possible then that settles it.

Fear corrupts the soul of man. Whoever the Son sets free is free indeed. You are free! The power of fear was broken and destroyed at the cross of Calvary. You are no longer a slave to fear, you are a child of God!

Rise up and enforce your victory. Do not give up the fight. You are a winner! Declare with conviction: *I am free from the power of fear!*

For more information or for booking enquires,
please contact

Email: elizabeth@ukwet.org